FIRST PEOPLES

CHEYENNE

VALERIE BODDEN

CREATIVE EDUCATION ✖ CREATIVE PAPERBACKS

Published by Creative Education and Creative Paperbacks
P.O. Box 227, Mankato, Minnesota 56002
Creative Education and Creative Paperbacks are imprints of
The Creative Company
www.thecreativecompany.us

Design by Christine Vanderbeek
Production by Colin O'Dea
Art direction by Rita Marshall
Printed in the United States of America

Photographs by Alamy (The Protected Art Archive, Rosanne
Tackaberry), Creative Commons Wikimedia (Karl Bodmer/
Library of Congress, George Catlin/Smithsonian American
Art Museum, John C. H. Grabill/Library of Congress, Edgar
Samuel Paxson/Buffalo Bill Center of the West/Whitney
Gallery of Western Art), Getty Images (Buyenlarge, Michael
Smith, Universal History Archive/UIG), iStockphoto
(KenCanning, robertcicchetti), Shutterstock (Miloje, Emre
Tarimcioglu)

Library of Congress Cataloging-in-Publication Data
Names: Bodden, Valerie, author.
Title: Cheyenne / Valerie Bodden.
Series: First peoples.
Includes bibliographical references and index.
Summary: An introduction to the Cheyenne lifestyle and
history, including their forced relocation and how they keep
traditions alive today. A Cheyenne story recounts how people
became chief of the animals.
Identifiers:
ISBN 978-1-64026-223-2 (hardcover)
ISBN 978-1-62832-786-1 (pbk)
ISBN 978-1-64000-358-3 (eBook)
This title has been submitted for CIP processing under LCCN
2019938364.
CCSS: RI.1.1, 2, 3, 4, 5, 6, 7; RI.2.1, 2, 3, 4, 5, 6; RI.3.1, 2, 3, 5;
RF.1.1, 3, 4; RF.2.3, 4

First Edition HC   9 8 7 6 5 4 3 2 1
First Edition PBK   9 8 7 6 5 4 3 2 1

FIRST PEOPLES

TABLE *of* CONTENTS

PEOPLE OF THE PLAINS

The Cheyenne lived on the GREAT PLAINS. The name *Cheyenne* came from a Sioux Indian word. It meant "people of a different speech." The Cheyenne called themselves *Tsitsistas*. This meant "the people."

 The Cheyenne were farmers before they moved to the Great Plains.

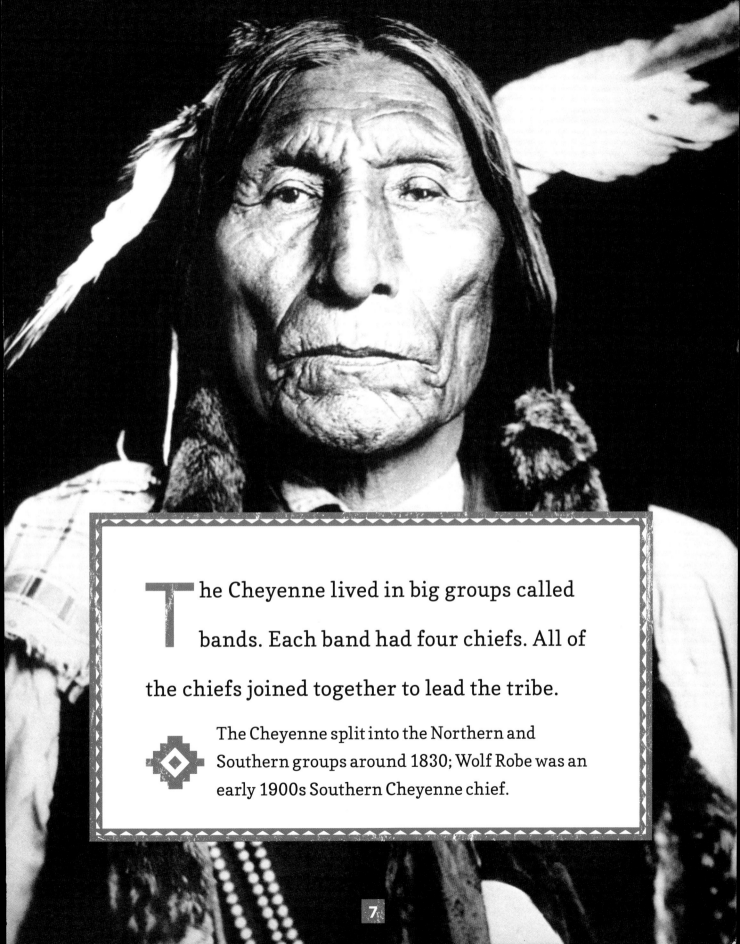

The Cheyenne lived in big groups called bands. Each band had four chiefs. All of the chiefs joined together to lead the tribe.

The Cheyenne split into the Northern and Southern groups around 1830; Wolf Robe was an early 1900s Southern Cheyenne chief.

CHEYENNE LIFE

The Cheyenne lived in tepees. Tepees were made of wooden poles and bison skins. They were easy to set up and take down. The Cheyenne did not stay in one place for long. They moved around to hunt bison.

 Flaps at the top of a tepee were opened to let out smoke from the fire or closed to keep out rain.

Cheyenne men hunted bison from horseback. They fought in wars. They used bows and arrows and sharp, long-handled lances. The men also went on raids to steal horses.

 Riding horses allowed the Cheyenne to hunt farther from home and bring back more meat.

Women gathered wild plants like berries and roots to eat. They were in charge of the tepee. They cooked meals and carried water to camp. They made all of the family's clothes.

 The Cheyenne spent the summer in small family camps but joined in larger groups for the winter.

CHEYENNE CEREMONIES

The Cheyenne believed in many GODS. They held CEREMONIES. In one, the whole tribe had to be quiet for four days.

 Most ceremonies, including the Sacred Arrow Renewal, took place during the summer.

SETTLERS AND RESERVATIONS

The Cheyenne met **SETTLERS** in the late 1600s. At first, things were peaceful. But then more settlers crossed Cheyenne land. Fights broke out between the Cheyenne and settlers.

 Cheyenne warriors joined other Plains tribes to fight the U.S. Army in the Battle of the Little Big Horn.

By the 1880s, the Cheyenne were forced to move to RESERVATIONS. Life was hard there. Many Cheyenne died of hunger and sickness.

 For many years, Cheyenne living on reservations were not allowed to hold ceremonies.

BEING CHEYENNE

Today, many Cheyenne still live on reservations. They hold ceremonies. Some still speak the musical Cheyenne language. They work to keep their TRADITIONS alive.

 Cheyenne and other tribes perform dances and music while wearing the traditional clothing of their people.

A CHEYENNE STORY

The Cheyenne told stories to explain their way of life. In one story, Bison was the strongest animal. He wanted to be chief. But the people also wanted to be chief. So they had a race. The winner would be chief. All animals with four legs were on Bison's team. The birds were on the people's team. Bison almost won the race. But a small bird zoomed ahead. She won! People became chief of the animals.

GLOSSARY

CEREMONIES ⟩ special acts carried out according to set rules

GODS ⟩ beings that people believe have special powers and control the world

GREAT PLAINS ⟩ grasslands stretching across much of western North America east of the Rocky Mountains

RESERVATIONS ⟩ areas of land set aside for American Indians

SETTLERS ⟩ people who come to live in a new area

TRADITIONS ⟩ beliefs, stories, or ways of doing things that are passed down from parents to their children

READ MORE

Fullman, Joe. *Native North Americans: Dress, Eat, Write, and Play Just Like the Native Americans*. Mankato, Minn.: QEB, 2010.

Morris, Ting. *Arts and Crafts of the Native Americans*. North Mankato, Minn.: Smart Apple Media, 2007.

WEBSITES

Common Cheyenne Words
http://wleman.tripod.com/sounds/soundfiles.htm
Learn how to spell and say words from the Cheyenne language.

National Park Service: Sand Creek Massacre National Historic Site
https://www.nps.gov/sand/learn/historyculture/people.htm
Learn about a Cheyenne battle and Cheyenne chiefs.

Note: Every effort has been made to ensure that the websites listed above are suitable for children, that they have educational value, and that they contain no inappropriate material. However, because of the nature of the Internet, it is impossible to guarantee that these sites will remain active indefinitely or that their contents will not be altered.

INDEX